This book is officially licensed by Winning Moves UK Ltd, owners
of the Top Trumps registered trademark.

Tim Dykes and Nick Judd have asserted their right to be
identified as the authors of this book.

First published in November 2008.

British Library Cataloguing-in-Publication Data:
A catalogue record for this book is available from
the British Library

ISBN 1 84425 646 4

Library of Congress catalog card no. 2008929399

Published by Haynes Publishing,
Sparkford, Yeovil, Somerset BA22 7JJ, UK
Tel: 01963 442030 Fax: 01963 440001
Int. tel: +44 1963 442030 Int. fax: +44 1963 440001
Email: sales@haynes.co.uk
Website: www.haynes.co.uk

Haynes North America, Inc.,
861 Lawrence Drive, Newbury Park
California 91320, USA

Design and layout by Richard Parsons

All photographs courtesy of Empics

Printed and bound in Great Britain by
J. H. Haynes & Co. Ltd, Sparkford

The Authors

After hanging up his one remaining boot following
an Eduardo-style injury, Nick Judd is hoping that his
beloved Swindon Town will one day groom a player
good enough to grace these pages. Southampton fan
Tim Dykes still regularly plays five-a-side, despite being
heavier than anyone in this book.

TOP TRUMPS

WORLD FOOTBALL STARS

2

Contents

About
Top Trumps

It's now more than 30 years since Britain's kids first caught the Top Trumps craze. The game remained hugely popular until the 1990s, when it slowly drifted into obscurity. Then, in 1999, UK games company Winning Moves discovered it, bought it, dusted it down, gave it a thorough makeover and introduced it to a whole new generation. And so the Top Trumps legend continues.

Nowadays, there are Top Trumps titles for just about everyone, with subjects about animals, cars, ships, aircraft and all the great films and TV shows. Top Trumps is now even more popular than before. In Britain, a pack of Top Trumps is bought every six seconds! And it's not just British children who love the game. Children in Australasia, the Far East, the Middle East, all over Europe and in North America can buy Top Trumps at their local shops.

Today you can even play the game on the internet, interactive DVD, your games console and even your mobile phone.

You've played the game...

Now read the book!

Haynes Publishing and Top Trumps have teamed up to bring you this exciting new Top Trumps book, in which you will find even more pictures, facts and ratings.

Top Trumps: World Football Stars features another 90 of the finest footballers on the planet, from Andrei Arshavin to Yuri Zhirkov, including emerging heroes like Alexandre Pato and Theo Walcott. Packed with facts and photographs, this is the essential pocket guide for football fans everywhere. Detailed biographies accompany statistics including a breakdown of each player's league appearances and goals at club level, as well as on the international stage (as of 1 August 2008).

Look out for other Top Trumps books from Haynes Publishing – even more facts, even more fun!

Emmanuel Adebayor
Togo

DoB	26 February 1984
Height	1.90m
Weight	70kg
Position	Striker
Togo	37 caps
	16 goals
Arsenal	78 league games
	36 goals
Transfer fee	£3million

Pace, power and clinical finishing combine to make Emmanuel Adebayor one of the most sought-after strikers in the game. Snapped up by Metz as a teenager, the Togolese target man bagged 15 Ligue 1 goals to earn a move to AS Monaco. There, he was part of the side which reached the Champions League final in 2004 and after scoring nine goals the following season, he joined Arsenal for £3million. The giant striker's career truly took off when the Gunners moved to the Emirates stadium in 2006, since when he has scored 32 goals in 65 Premier League matches.

Igor Akinfeev
Russia

DoB	8 April 1986
Height	1.83m
Weight	71kg
Position	Goalkeeper
Russia	25 caps
	0 goals
CSKA	116 league games
Moscow	0 goals
Transfer fee	n/a

After being handed his debut as a 17-year-old, Igor Akinfeev is far more experienced than his age suggests, having made his 100th Russian Premier-Liga appearance for CSKA Moscow on his 21st birthday. During his first six seasons with the Army Men, Akinfeev won three Russian titles and the 2004/05 UEFA Cup – keeping clean sheets in all four home ties en route to the final. The following season he went 362 minutes of CSKA's Champions League campaign before conceding a goal. He returned from a knee ligament injury to star as Russia marched to the semi-finals at Euro 2008.

Massimo Ambrosini
Italy

DoB	29 May 1977
Height	1.80m
Weight	67kg
Position	Midfielder
Italy	35 caps
	0 goals
AC Milan	226 league games
	19 goals
Transfer fee	n/a

Blessed with an incredible engine, hard-running Massimo Ambrosini is the textbook defensive midfielder. Aerially strong and ferocious in the tackle, Ambrosini is now vice-captain of AC Milan – but it took time to establish himself in the side. Following a solid debut season with Cesena in Serie B, Milan coach Fabio Capello took him to the San Siro in 1998 with high hopes. But it was only after a spectacular breakthrough campaign on loan at Vicenza that Ambrosini became a first-choice midfielder at Milan, helping the Rossoneri to two European Cup finals and winning 35 international caps along the way.

Anderson
Brazil

DoB	13 April 1988
Height	1.76m
Weight	69kg
Position	Midfielder
Brazil	7 caps
	0 goals
Manchester United	24 league games
	0 goals
Transfer fee	Undisclosed

Few Manchester United fans had heard of their new man following his move from FC Porto in 2007. Fans rushed to websites with one clip featuring an incredible solo match-winning goal for first club Gremio after his side had been reduced to seven players. Brought in initially as a long-term replacement for Paul Scholes, Anderson was given an early chance to impress. He took it, making 38 all-competition appearances in a debut season that featured Premier League and European Cup winners' medals. His box-to-box exploits prove he is a match for the most talented midfielders in England.

Nicolas Anelka
France

DoB	14 March 1979
Height	1.85m
Weight	82kg
Position	Striker
France	51 caps
	10 goals
Chelsea	14 league games
	1 goal
Transfer fee	£15million

Nicolas Anelka is the most expensive footballer in history after commanding more than £85million in transfer fees. His move from Bolton Wanderers to Chelsea in January 2008 was his eighth move in 10 years. The deadly striker started his career at Paris St Germain before Arsene Wenger took him to Highbury in 1997. He won the PFA Player of the Year award in 1999, but signed for Real Madrid before returning to his first club. In 2002 he joined Liverpool before moving to Manchester City, where he scored 38 goals in 89 games. A move to Fenerbahce preceded his move to Stamford Bridge.

Aleksandr Anyukov
Russia

DoB	28 September 1982
Height	1.75m
Weight	65kg
Position	Defender
Russia	37 caps
	1 goal
Zenit	66 league games
St Petersburg	6 goals
Transfer fee	Undisclosed

Quick, uncompromising right wing-back Aleksandr Anyukov was part of the Zenit St Petersburg side which lifted the UEFA Cup in 2007/08 – two years after reaching the quarter-finals of the same competition. Samara-born Anyukov began his career for local side Krylia Sovetov, helping them reach the Russian Premier-Liga and forcing his way into the national squad for Euro 2004 before being snapped up by Zenit midway through the following season. He helped his new club win the title in 2007 – scoring twice in the process – and played all five games as Russia reached the last four at Euro 2008.

Alberto Aquilani
Italy

DoB	7 July 1984
Height	1.84m
Weight	78kg
Position	Midfielder
Italy	7 caps
	0 goals
AS Roma	88 league games
	7 goals
Transfer fee	n/a

Solid technique, composed passing and venomous long-range shooting combine to make Alberto Aquilani one of the game's most sought-after young midfielders. Born in the Italian capital, Aquilani turned down a contract offer from Chelsea to sign for his boyhood idols Roma, where he came of age after a full season on loan at Serie B side Triestina. Aquilani made 88 Serie A appearances in his first four seasons with the Giallorossi first team and has won seven Italian caps, the last of which came as a replacement for the suspended Andrea Pirlo in the Azzurri's Euro 2008 quarter-final defeat to eventual winners Spain.

Andrei Arshavin
Russia

DoB	29 May 1981
Height	1.72m
Weight	62kg
Position	Forward
Russia	37 caps
	12 goals
Zenit	217 league games
St Petersburg	47 goals
Transfer fee	n/a

Born in St Petersburg, gifted playmaker Andrei Arshavin has been at local club Zenit since he was 17, making over 200 Russian Premier League appearances. His most successful campaign to date was unquestionably 2007/08, during which time the dynamo scored 10 goals to help Zenit to their first Russian Premier-Liga title before starring as they swept aside all before them in the UEFA Cup. Showcasing his two quick feet and superb vision, Arshavin shone at Euro 2008, returning from a two-match suspension to score one goal and make another in Russia's memorable victories over Sweden and Holland.

Ryan Babel
Holland

DoB	19 December 1986
Height	1.84m
Weight	79kg
Position	Forward
Holland	25 caps
	5 goals
Liverpool	30 league games
	4 goals
Transfer fee	£11.5million

KNVB

Liverpool winger Ryan Babel has been described by club legend Kenny Dalglish as a player who "will terrify players in the Premier League." He won Liverpool's Young Player of the Year award in his debut season after scoring 10 goals in 48 appearances following his move to Anfield in 2007. Babel started his career representing Ajax's various youth teams before he signed professional terms in 2004. He won an Eredivisie winners' medal in his first season and scored the winning goal in the Dutch Super Cup against PSV Eindhoven a year later, an honour he helped the club retain in 2006.

Tranquillo Barnetta
Switzerland

DoB	22 May 1985
Height	1.76m
Weight	62kg
Position	Midfielder
Switzerland	35 caps
	6 goals
Bayer Leverkusen	93 league games
	13 goals
Transfer fee	n/a

Direct but unafraid to play with a flourish, attacking midfielder Tranquillo Barnetta stood out in a disappointing Switzerland team at Euro 2008. The Bayer Leverkusen player, who began at St Gallen before adjusting to the Bundesliga during a loan spell at Hannover, was at the heart of everything positive the Swiss produced in the tournament's opening game. Close control at pace and accurate delivery from the flanks make Barnetta a popular player with fans and teammates alike – and after recovering from cruciate ligament damage, he has ensured his name is one of the first on the Leverkusen team sheet each week.

Gareth Barry
England

DoB	23 February 1981
Height	1.80m
Weight	78kg
Position	Midfielder
England	20 caps
	1 goal
Aston Villa	327 league games
	36 goals
Transfer fee	n/a

ENGLAND

Liverpool spent the summer chasing England regular Gareth Barry but could not meet Aston Villa's £18million valuation of their frustrated captain. Barry boasts 20 caps and alongside David Beckham, is the only other international to have played under every England manager since first selected by Kevin Keegan. Barry joined Villa as a trainee centre back and switched to the left before impressing in the centre of midfield. In October 2007, aged 26 years and 247 days, he became the youngest player to appear in 300 Premier League games.

ENGLAND
v
ESTONIA
13.10.2007

David Bentley
England

DoB	27 August 1984
Height	1.75m
Weight	68kg
Position	Midfielder
England	6 caps
	0 goals
Tottenham Hotspur	0 league games
	0 goals
Transfer fee	£15million

ENGLAND

David Bentley joined Tottenham in 2008 for an initial fee of £15million after the Peterborough-born winger enjoyed a meteoric rise at Blackburn Rovers. Bentley ended 2006/07 with seven goals and 13 assists and a Player of the Year award. Eight goals and 13 more assists followed in 2007/08, bringing six international appearances. Bentley spent five years at Arsenal but failed to make a serious breakthrough, instead joining Norwich City and Rovers on loan. He joined the latter permanently in 2006, scoring a hat-trick against Manchester United, the youngest player in Premier League history to do so against Sir Alex Ferguson's side.

Karim Benzema
France

DoB	17 December 1987
Height	1.83m
Weight	73kg
Position	Striker
France	13 caps
	3 goals
Lyon	76 league games
	26 goals
Transfer fee	n/a

It is little wonder that Karim Benzema was recently voted the best player in France. In the 2007/08 season, the striker averaged more than a goal every other game for Olympique Lyonnais, with whom he won his fourth successive Ligue 1 title. Benzema – who now plays in attack but can also play on the wing – is a product of the French champions' youth academy. In 2006/07 he scored seven goals in 24 games as the main striker, earning himself a call-up to the national side. Benzema's power, precision, speed and accuracy saw him selected for Les Bleus' ill-fated Euro 2008 squad.

Artur Boruc
Poland

DoB	20 February 1980
Height	1.93m
Weight	85kg
Position	Goalkeeper
Poland	37 caps
	0 goals
Celtic	100 league games
	0 goals
Transfer fee	Undisclosed

Brave, agile and acrobatic, Artur Boruc has been Poland's first-choice goalkeeper since 2005, when he left his boyhood idols Legia Warsaw for a loan move to Celtic. The Glasgow side soon made the deal permanent and Boruc duly helped the Hoops win three consecutive Scottish Premier League titles – as well as reaching the Champions League knockout stages in 2007 and 2008. Despite those achievements – and representing his country at the 2006 World Cup – Boruc's proudest moment came as a 24-year-old at Legia, when he scored the only goal of his career with a penalty against Widzew Lodz.

Jose Bosingwa
Portugal

DoB	24 August 1982
Height	1.83m
Weight	75kg
Position	Defender
Portugal	11 caps
	0 goals
Chelsea	0 league games
	0 goals
Transfer fee	£16.3million

Portuguese full-back Jose Bosingwa was promptly joined by his national team boss Luiz Felipe Scolari at Stamford Bridge after his £16.3million switch from Porto in the summer of 2008. He had helped the Portugese side complete a hat-trick of titles before departing for the Premier League. The pacy defender was a fringe player in former Porto boss José Mourinho's winning 2003/04 Champions League squad – but under Co Adriaanse and later Jesualdo Ferreira, Bosingwa evolved into an international regular. Since his debut in a 2–1 Euro 2008 qualifier win in Belgium, he has gone on to make a further 10 appearances.

Michael Carrick
England

DoB	27 July 1981
Height	1.82m
Weight	74kg
Position	Midfielder
England	14 caps
	0 goals
Manchester	64 league games
United	5 goals
Transfer fee	£14million

ENGLAND

An increasingly integral part of Manchester United's line-up, understated Geordie Michael Carrick goes about his business quietly and effectively. It's no coincidence that United have won back-to-back titles with Carrick at the fulcrum of their midfield. A consistent passer of the ball, Carrick can split a defence and while England boss Fabio Capello has so far overlooked him, Sir Alex Ferguson often picks him ahead of Paul Scholes, Owen Hargreaves or Anderson. A Wallsend Boys Club graduate, Carrick developed his trade at West Ham United's youth academy and first team before joining Tottenham Hotspur in 2004. He moved to United in 2006.

Giorgio Chiellini
Italy

DoB	14 August 1984
Height	1.86m
Weight	76kg
Position	Defender
Italy	13 caps
	1 goal
Juventus	79 league games
	6 goals
Transfer fee	£5.6million

The latest in a long line of world-class Italian defenders, Giorgio Chiellini blossomed at Euro 2008, producing flawless performances against France and Spain before the Azzurri's quarter-final defeat on penalties. Positionally superb, Chiellini reads the game like a veteran and has an eye for goal, too; averaging a goal every 13 league games. He began his career at Livorno before being bought by Juventus, and immediately part sold on to Fiorentina. Composed performances for the Viola brought Chiellini international recognition – and prompted Juve to pay for complete ownership of the player, who is now an integral part of the Bianconeri defence.

Cristian Chivu
Romania

DoB	15 October 1980
Height	1.83m
Weight	78kg
Position	Defender
Romania	62 caps
	3 goals
Inter Milan	26 league games
	0 goals
Transfer fee	£10.07million

Uncompromising yet composed defender Cristian Chivu is a rock at the back for Italian champions Inter Milan. Plucked from the relative obscurity of Romanian football by Ajax in 1999, Chivu was soon hitting the headlines. The versatile, left-footed defender scored in his country's 3–2 win over England at Euro 2000, helped Ajax win the Dutch league and cup double in 2002, then made a reported £12million move to Roma a year later. Chivu, who can take a mean free-kick, racked up 85 Serie A appearances for the Giallorossi before Inter paid more than £10m for his services in 2007.

Joe Cole
England

DoB	7 November 1981
Height	1.75m
Weight	69kg
Position	Midfielder
England	50 caps
	7 goals
Chelsea	143 league games
	23 goals
Transfer fee	£6.6million

ENGLAND

One of England's most exciting attacking midfielders, Cole can operate on either flank or behind the strikers. The London-born trickster came through West Ham United's successful youth academy and was made first-team captain aged just 21. But after the Hammers were relegated in 2003, he joined Chelsea. Cole struggled under Claudio Ranieri but improved vastly under Jose Mourinho's tutelage, despite the Portuguese claiming Cole had "two faces", one of which didn't like defending. He won back-to-back league titles in 2005 and 2006 but enjoyed his best season in 2007/08, when Blues fans voted him their Player of the Year.

Volkan Demirel
Turkey

DoB	27 October 1981
Height	1.91m
Weight	92kg
Position	Goalkeeper
Turkey	24 caps
	0 goals
Fenerbahce	85 league games
	0 goals
Transfer fee	n/a

Resilient, agile and blessed with quick reflexes, Fenerbahce goalkeeper Volkan Demirel rounded off a majestic campaign at club level by helping Turkey shock their way to the semi-finals at Euro 2008 in Austria and Switzerland. The flamboyant custodian became Turkey's first choice after a superb season at the Sukru Saracoglu, notably producing three saves in a penalty shoot-out victory over Sevilla to help Fenerbahce reach the Champions League quarter-finals. With three Turkish titles under his belt, Volkan travelled to Euro 2008 full of confidence – and despite being sent off against the Czech Republic, he returned home a hero.

Daniele De Rossi
Italy

DoB	24 July 1984
Height	1.83m
Weight	76kg
Position	Midfielder
Italy	36 caps
	5 goals
AS Roma	155 league games
	17 goals
Transfer fee	n/a

Capped 36 times for his country since playing an integral part in Italy's victory at the European Under-21 Championship in 2004, gritty midfielder Daniele De Rossi has spent his whole career at hometown club Roma. He made his Serie A debut for the Giallorossi as a 19-year-old and is now widely considered to be a ready-made replacement for Roma stalwart Francesco Totti. At international level, De Rossi was infamously sent off at the 2006 World Cup for elbowing United States striker Brian McBride but returned from suspension to score in the Azzurri's penalty shoot-out victory over France in the final.

Mahamadou Diarra

Mali

DoB	18 May 1981
Height	1.83m
Weight	76kg
Position	Midfielder
Mali	22 caps
	5 goals
Real Madrid	63 league games
	3 goals
Transfer fee	£17.7million

Five consecutive Ligue 1 titles with Lyon convinced Real Madrid to pay £17.7million for Mahamadou Diarra – and his arrival duly helped Los Merengues end their long wait for a trophy. The defensive midfielder's header against Real Mallorca on the last day of the season essentially clinched the La Liga title – and Diarra was an integral part of the side which regained that silverware in 2007/08. After starting his career with Greek side OFI Crete and Dutch outfit Vitesse, Diarra's supreme fitness, work rate and combative nature combine to make the Mali captain a transfer target for the world's richest clubs.

Diego
Brazil

DoB	28 February 1985
Height	1.73m
Weight	73kg
Position	Midfielder
Brazil	31 caps
	4 goals
Werder	63 league games
Bremen	26 goals
Transfer fee	£4.08million

A star at Werder Bremen, who he joined from FC Porto in 2006, the attacking No.10 started so well at his new club that, together with fellow midfielder Torsten Frings, he was dubbed one of "two motors of Bremen's midfield" by the German press. A regular Player of the Month, Diego is yet to win the Bundesliga title, yet he has enjoyed plenty of success for his country. He made his international debut in the Copa America in 2004 and scored in the penalty shootout against Argentina in the final to help secure his first of two Copa America winners' medals.

Antonio Di Natale
Italy

DoB	13 October 1977
Height	1.77m
Weight	70kg
Position	Striker
Italy	20 caps
	7 goals
Udinese	135 league games
	43 goals
Transfer fee	Player exchange

A product of Empoli's youth system, Napoli-born Antonio Di Natale grew up watching his hero Diego Maradona – and is himself a classic example of a smaller, fleet-footed striker who plays off the shoulder of a centre-forward. He made 159 league appearances for the Tuscany side, attracting the attention of Giovanni Trapattoni, the national team coach at the time, and of Udinese, who acquired him in a swap deal in 2004. His goals helped the Zebrette to their best Serie A finish in seven years and a place in the Champions League. He has been an integral part of the set-up ever since.

Giovani dos Santos
Mexico

DoB	**11 May 1989**
Height	**1.75m**
Weight	**74kg**
Position	**Midfielder**
Mexico	**5 caps**
	0 goals
Tottenham	**0 caps**
	0 goals
Transfer fee	**£4.78million**

The latest Mexican teenager to be burdened with the tag "the new Hugo Sanchez", Giovani dos Santos shot to fame at the Under-17 World Championship in 2005. The attacking midfielder provided eight assists as his country stormed to the title, beating Brazil 3–0 in the final. Blessed with pace, great touch and superb vision, Dos Santos flourished again two summers later, scoring three goals at the Under-20 World Championship. Despite a hat-trick for Barcelona against Real Murcia, first-team opportunities were limited at the Nou Camp and the teenager moved to Tottenham for an initial £4.78million fee in June 2008.

Royston Drenthe
Holland

DoB	8 April 1987
Height	1.82m
Weight	78kg
Position	Midfielder
Holland	0 caps
	0 goals
Real Madrid	18 league games
	2 goals
Transfer fee	£10million

KNVB

Royston Drenthe experienced disciplinary problems while at Feyenoord's youth academy and subsequently joined Excelsior Rotterdam. There he impressed in the left-back position and duly returned to Feyenoord, where he continued to excel. After rising from the reserves to the A team he was soon made first-team captain. A fans' favourite, he became a target for a host of European clubs after he was named player of the tournament at the European Under-21 football Championships in 2007. Drenthe opted for Real Madrid and signed along with Wesley Sneijder, helping Los Merengues clinch the title in his first season at the Bernabeu.

Elano
Brazil

DoB	14 June 1981
Height	1.74m
Weight	65kg
Position	Midfielder
Brazil	22 caps
	4 goals
Manchester City	34 league games
	8 goals
Transfer fee	£8million

Few had heard of Elano before Manchester City signed the Brazilian in 2007; by the season's end he had established himself as one of the Premier League's brightest midfielders. Elano joined Shakhtar Donestsk from Santos in 2005 – where he racked up 14 league goals in 48 games – and became the first player to represent Brazil while playing in the Ukrainian league. The roving midfielder with an eye for goal, who has hit the target four times in 22 appearances for his country, settled quickly in Manchester after his £8million move and finished his first campaign with eight goals.

Patrice Evra
France

DoB	15 May 1981
Height	1.75m
Weight	76kg
Position	Defender
France	13 caps
	0 goals
Manchester	68 league games
United	1 goal
Transfer fee	£5.5million

Powerhouse defender Patrice Evra is revered for his strength in the tackle, passion and desire to make rampaging runs. One of 26 siblings, Evra was born in Senegal before moving to France as a child. He developed his game in Italy with Marsala and Monza before returning 'home' for spells at Nice and Monaco, for whom he made 120 Ligue 1 appearances and played in the 2004 Champions League final. Floored by a Porto side featuring Ricardo Carvalho on that occasion, Evra had the last laugh when Manchester United, who he joined for £5.5million in 2006, beat Carvalho and Chelsea in the 2008 final.

Jefferson Farfan

Peru

DoB	28 October 1984
Height	1.74m
Weight	72kg
Position	Striker
Peru	41 caps
	12 goals
Schalke 04	0 league games
	0 goals
Transfer fee	£11.09million

A consistently high goalscoring record persuaded Schalke 04 to pay £11.09million for robust centre-forward Jefferson Farfan in the summer of 2008. Described by Schalke boss Andreas Muller as "a very solid player", the powerhouse striker smashed in 57 league goals in four seasons with PSV Eindhoven – helping the club win three consecutive Dutch titles. As a teenager, Farfan averaged exactly a goal every other game in his last two seasons with Alianza Lima – prompting PSV to make their move. He made his international debut as an 18-year-old and finished the 2006 World Cup qualifying campaign as the second-highest goalscorer.

Mathieu Flamini

France

DoB	7 March 1984
Height	1.78m
Weight	67kg
Position	Midfielder
France	2 caps
	0 goals
AC Milan	0 league games
	0 goals
Transfer fee	Free

An impressive defensive midfielder who started life at hometown club Marseille, Mathieu Flamini left Arsenal in 2008 after having spent four years in north London. Flamini went from being a utility player – often at left-back in the 2004/05 campaign – to an integral part of the Gunners' midfield. The 2007/08 campaign was his best. He forged a promising relationship with Cesc Fabregas and scored one of the goals of the season; a thunderous 23-metre strike in a 3–0 win over Newcastle United. Flamini has made just two international appearances, but his move to AC Milan could help increase that tally.

Alexander Frei
Switzerland

DoB	15 July 1979
Height	1.79m
Weight	69kg
Position	Striker
Switzerland	60 caps
	35 goals
Borussia Dortmund	45 league games
	22 goals
Transfer fee	£2.76million

One of the most consistent goalscorers in Europe, Switzerland captain Alexander Frei has been a success everywhere he has played. The striker made his name at Servette, scoring 36 goals in 64 games and helping the unfashionable side reach the last 16 of the UEFA Cup in 2001/02. A move to French outfit Rennes brought 46 goals in 100 Ligue 1 matches and drew the attention of Borussia Dortmund, who paid £2.76million for the robust front-runner's goalscoring ability in 2006. A thigh problem restricted Frei in 2007/08 and his frustration grew when he hobbled out of Euro 2008 with a knee injury.

Alberto Gilardino
Italy

DoB	5 July 1982
Height	1.84m
Weight	78kg
Position	Striker
Italy	25 caps
	9 goals
Fiorentina	0 caps
	0 goals
Transfer fee	£11.15million

Italian international striker Alberto Gilardino started making the headlines in the 2003/04 season, when he racked up 23 goals for Parma and then finished as joint-top scorer as Italy won the European Under-21 Championship. Another 23-goal season from the broad-chested front man earned Gilardino a place in Italy's 2006 World Cup winning squad and a €24million move to AC Milan, with whom he won the Champions League in 2007. Having played under Cesare Prandelli at Verona and Parma, Gilardino agreed to once again link up with the legendary Juventus midfielder, now coaching Fiorentina, after signing a £11.15m deal in May 2008.

Mario Gomez
Germany

DoB	10 July 1985
Height	1.89m
Weight	86kg
Position	Striker
Germany	14 caps
	6 goals
Stuttgart	89 league games
	39 goals
Transfer fee	n/a

Six goals in 14 games is an impressive return for a youngster beginning his international career and while rampaging striker Mario Gomez failed to score at Euro 2008, many still predict a bright future. The Stuttgart centre-forward established himself as a regular scorer in Die Roten's 2006/07 Bundesliga-winning campaign. By the end of the season, despite numerous injuries, he had been crowned German Footballer of the Year and scored on his international debut against Switzerland. A year later he had added a further 19 league goals, second only to Bayern Munich's Luca Toni in the Bundesliga goalscoring charts.

Bafetimbi Gomis

France

DoB	6 August 1985
Height	1.84m
Weight	77kg
Position	Striker
France	4 caps
	2 goals
St Étienne	106 league games
	30 goals
Transfer fee	n/a

Bafetimbi Gomis started life at St Étienne but was sent on loan to Troyes to gain experience in 2005. He scored six times in 13 appearances and returned to Les Verts in 2006 full of confidence, scoring 10 goals in his first season back at the Geoffroy-Guichard. In 2007/08 he recorded his most impressive goals haul – 16 goals in 35 games – which saw him called up to Raymond Domenech's Euro 2008 squad ahead of David Trezeguet. In a warm-up match against Ecuador in May, he became only the second French player after Zinedine Zidane to score twice on their international debut.

Johnny Heitinga

Holland

DoB	15 November 1983
Height	1.80m
Weight	72kg
Position	Defender
Holland	39 caps
	5 goals
Atletico Madrid	0 league games
	0 goals
Transfer fee	£8million

KNVB

Johnny Heitinga established himself in the Ajax first team following a solid debut against rivals Feyenoord in 2001. The versatile defender was unlucky with injuries in his first three seasons, but after a regular run in 2003/04 – in which Ajax won the Eredivisie – he soon caught the eye of Holland coach Dick Advocaat. He made his senior debut against the USA in 2004 and has since earned 39 caps, scoring five goals. Injury hampered the 2005/06 season but a return to form saw Heitinga named Dutch Player of the Year in April 2008. Atletico Madrid duly offered the £8million required to trigger Heitinga's release clause, and he joined the Spanish outfit in June 2008.

Alexander Hleb
Belarus

DoB	1 May 1981
Height	1.78m
Weight	69kg
Position	Midfielder
Belarus	41 caps
	4 goals
Barcelona	0 league games
	0 goals
Transfer fee	£11.9million

A star in Belarus, Alexander Hleb has spent the last three seasons deployed on Arsenal's right flank. He came to prominence at VfB Stuttgart, who he joined in 2000. He quickly became the side's playmaker and his consistency saw him named Belarus' Player of the Year five years out of six. Nicknamed 'The Magician', he boasted the most assists in the Bundesliga in his last season before moving to Arsenal in 2005, where he scored seven goals in 89 Premier League appearances. Boasting excellent balance and a low centre of gravity, Hleb was sold to Barcelona for £11.9million in July 2008.

Andres Iniesta
Spain

DoB	11 May 1984
Height	1.70m
Weight	72kg
Position	Midfielder
Spain	29 caps
	4 goals
Barcelona	155 league games
	12 goals
Transfer fee	n/a

International success was always on the cards for Andres Iniesta, who played a pivotal role in Spain winning the European Under-16 Championship in 2001, and the Under-19 version a year later. Talented midfielder Iniesta finally made the step up to the national side in 2006 – and is now an established part of the dazzling midfield unit, playing a full game as Spain beat Germany to win Euro 2008. Nevertheless, his quick thinking and passing was not as evident as it has been for Barcelona, with whom the one-club man has won two La Liga titles and the 2006 Champions League.

Andreas Ivanschitz
Austria

DoB	15 October 1983
Height	1.79m
Weight	77kg
Position	Midfielder
Austria	42 caps
	6 goals
Panathinakos	50 league games
	7 goals
Transfer fee	£1.19million

Dubbed 'the Austrian David Beckham', Andreas Ivanschitz became Austria's youngest ever captain at 19 years and 361 days. Now 24, his creative left foot saw him impress in the centre of midfield during Euro 2008. He made his club debut for SK Rapid Wien aged 16 and went on to make 147 league appearances, scoring 25 goals. He won the Austrian Footballer of the Year award in 2003 and the Austrian Championship title two years later before joining Red Bull Salzburg in 2006. He joined Greek champions Panathinaikos on loan the same year before making the deal permanent in July 2008.

Marek Jankulovski
Czech Republic

DoB	9 May 1977
Height	1.83m
Weight	82kg
Position	Defender
Czech Republic	67 caps
	10 goals
AC Milan	69 league games
	4 goals
Transfer fee	Undisclosed

Voted Czech Player of the Year ahead of Peter Cech in 2007, defender Marek Jankulovski plays for Italian giants AC Milan. Born to a Macedonian father who later moved across the border to the Czech Republic, the 31-year-old has represented the Czechs at the last three European Championships, as well as the World Cup in 2006. He signed for the Rossoneri after spells at Napoli and Udinese, and he played in the UEFA Champions League final against Liverpool in 2006. He also scored the second goal in Milan's UEFA Super Cup victory against FC Sevilla in 2007.

Ivan Klasnic
Croatia

DoB	29 January 1980
Height	1.82m
Weight	76kg
Position	Striker
Croatia	31 caps
	10 goals
Nantes	0 league games
	0 goals
Transfer fee	Free

Ivan Klasnic scored twice at Euro 2008 but it was remarkable to see him playing at all, given he had only just recovered from a kidney transplant. Born in Hamburg, Klasnic turned down both Germany and Bosnia and Herzegovina, deciding instead to represent Croatia, for whom he's scored 10 goals in 31 internationals. He started his domestic career at St Pauli in 1998, making most of his 95 Bundesliga appearances for the club before turning 21. He joined Werder Bremen in 2001, where he scored 49 league goals in 151 games before leaving for Nantes on a Bosman free transfer in 2008.

Niko Kranjcar
Croatia

DoB	13 August 1984
Height	1.84m
Weight	83kg
Position	Midfielder
Croatia	45 caps
	6 goals
Portsmouth	58 league games
	6 goals
Transfer fee	£3.5million

Described as a "magician" by Portsmouth team-mate Hermann Hreidarsson, Croatia's Niko Kranjcar is fast becoming one of the Premier League's most talented wingers. "He has created so many goals for us," continued Hreidersson. "He entertains the crowd, too." Son of Croatian legend Zlatko "Cico" Kranjcar, Niko impressed for Dinamo Zagreb and rivals Hadjuk Split before coming to the attention of fans the world over at the 2006 World Cup. His impressive performances led to Portsmouth securing his signature and in his second season he helped unfashionable Pompey win the FA Cup for the first time in 69 years.

Bojan Krkic
Spain

DoB	28 August 1990
Height	1.69m
Weight	62kg
Position	Striker
Spain	4 caps
Under-21	3 goals
Barcelona	31 league games
	10 goals
Transfer fee	n/a

The son of the former Red Star Belgrade player of the same name, red-hot striker Bojan Krkic has given Barcelona fans real hope for the future. Born in Catalonia, the diminutive frontman racked up 10 goals in 22 games for Barca's reserves before making his first-team bow in September 2007. He scored steadily when given the chance, but it was Bojan's spell of four goals in three matches which thrust the gifted finisher into the spotlight. National coach Luis Aragones included Bojan in his 23-man squad for the European Championship, but the youngster pulled out with fatigue. His time will come.

Manucho
Angola

DoB	7 March 1983
Height	1.88m
Weight	80kg
Position	Striker
Angola	14 caps
	6 goals
Manchester	0 league games
United	0 goals
Transfer fee	Undisclosed

Manucho – or Mateus Alberto Contreiras Concalves to give him his full moniker – rose to prominence after finishing top scorer in consecutive seasons in the Girabola, the Angolan national championship. He scored 16 goals in 2006, 15 a year later and Manchester United manager Sir Alex Ferguson signed him after he impressed in a three-week trial. Shortly after his move to Old Trafford he scored four goals for Angola in the African Nations Cup and finished in the team of the tournament. Shortly afterwards, he was sent on loan to Panathinaikos, Greece, where he scored on his debut against Larissa.

Carlos Marchena
Spain

DoB	31 July 1979
Height	1.83m
Weight	78kg
Position	Defender
Spain	47 caps
	2 goals
Valencia	180 league games
	5 goals
Transfer fee	Swap deal

Imposing centre-half Carlos Marchena first came to prominence as a teenager with Sevilla, who he helped gain promotion to the Spanish top-flight in 1999. Relegation the following year saw the defender opt for a switch to Benfica – but he returned to La Liga in 2001, joining Valencia while Zlatko Zahovic moved in the opposite direction. He lifted the Spanish title in his first season with Los Che, then won the league and UEFA Cup double two years later. After winning the Copa del Rey in 2008, he tasted success with the national team, playing a key role in Spain's Euro 2008 triumph.

Obafemi Martins
Nigeria

DoB	28 October 1984
Height	1.70m
Weight	70kg
Position	Striker
Nigeria	21 caps
	13 goals
Newcastle	64 league games
	20 goals
Transfer fee	£10.16million

An explosive striker, Obafemi Martins has twice been voted African Young Player of the Year and averages nearly two goals every three games for Nigeria. Pinched from the Reggiana youth set-up, Martins moved to Internazionale for £500,000 in 2000 – scoring seven Serie A goals mainly as a substitute in his breakthrough season. In August 2006, Martins was sold to Newcastle to make room for new signings Zlatan Ibrahimovic and Hernan Crespo. A knee injury hampered his start, but in his first two seasons at St James' Park, the Nigerian scored 27 goals in all competitions and soon became a firm fan favourite.

Javier Mascherano
Argentina

DoB	8 June 1984
Height	1.71m
Weight	66kg
Position	Midfielder
Argentina	41 caps
	2 goals
Liverpool	32 league games
	1 goal
Transfer fee	Undisclosed

Javier Mascherano boasts an Italian passport but has so far earned 41 caps for Argentina. In 2004 when he was voted the Albicelestes' best player in the Copa America. They lost in the final to Brazil, but he went one better later that year when he won an Olympic gold medal. His domestic career started with River Plate. A move to Corinthians followed, where he spent a year before a surprising switch to West Ham United took him to England. He made just five appearances at Upton Park before Liverpool bought his registration from the Media Sports Investments consortium in a controversial, protracted ownership issue.

Aiden McGeady
Republic of Ireland

DoB	4 April 1986
Height	1.77m
Weight	71kg
Position	Midfielder
Republic of Ireland	18 caps
	0 goals
Celtic	121 league games
	21 goals
Transfer fee	n/a

Nimble winger Aiden McGeady was born and raised in Glasgow but opted to play for the Republic of Ireland, the nation of his paternal grandfather, much to the disappointment of most Scottish fans. He joined Celtic as a schoolboy and turned down a move to Arsenal before making his Hoops debut shortly after his 18th birthday. McGeady scored in a 1–1 draw at Heart of Midlothian and went on to become a regular in the side, helping Celtic win three consecutive Scottish Premier League titles. His propensity for tricks, stepovers and spins saw him crowned Scottish Footballer of the Year in 2008.

Olof Mellberg
Sweden

DoB	3 September 1977
Height	1.84m
Weight	82kg
Position	Defender
Sweden	85 caps
	4 goals
Juventus	0 league games
	0 goals
Transfer fee	Free

Strong in the air and composed on the deck, versatile defender Olof Mellberg is one of the most experienced players in European football, having represented clubs in all three major leagues. Mellberg began in Sweden and won the championship with AIK at the age of 20 before joining Spanish strugglers Racing Santander. Despite the club's poor fortunes, Mellberg excelled in three years at the El Sardinero – earning the first of many Swedish caps prior to Euro 2000. Eight years – and five international tournaments – later, after making 232 Premier League appearances for Aston Villa, Mellberg joined Juventus on a Bosman free transfer.

Jeremy Menez

France

DoB	7 May 1987
Height	1.82m
Weight	73kg
Position	Forward
France	0 caps
	0 goals
Monaco	54 league games
	14 goals
Transfer fee	£2.39million

An attacking midfielder or striker, Jeremy Menez joined AS Monaco from Sochaux in 2006 after he formed part of the France side that won the 2003/04 UEFA European Under-17 Championship. He scored five goals at the Meridian Cup in Egypt and has since become an established member of the Under-19 and Under-21 set-up. Before joining Monaco, Menez scored seven goals in 55 league matches. He is the youngest ever scorer of a hat-trick in Ligue 1, the youngest winner of Ligue 1's player of the month award and he continues to attract attention from Europe's biggest clubs.

Per Mertesacker
Germany

DoB	29 September 1984
Height	1.96m
Weight	85kg
Position	Defender
Germany	49 caps
	1 goals
Werder Bremen	57 league games
	3 goals
Transfer fee	£3.38million

Despite his age, Per Mertesacker finished Euro 2008 within touching distance of his 50th German cap. He made his international debut 10 days after his 20th birthday under Jurgen Klinsmann, and he has since established himself alongside Christoph Metzelder in the centre of defence. The duo helped Germany reach the Euro 2008 final but after defeat to Spain, Mertesacker is yet to win an honour. Born in Hannover, Mertsesacker represented his home club and established himself as one of the Bundesliga's rising stars. He was dubbed "the Defence Pole" by German newspapers and his form ensured a £3.38million move to Werder Bremen in 2006.

Christoph Metzelder
Germany

DoB	5 November 1980
Height	1.93m
Weight	84kg
Position	Defender
Germany	47 caps
	0 goals
Real Madrid	9 league games
	0 goals
Transfer fee	Free

A Bundesliga champion with Borussia Dortmund at the age of 20, centre-half Christoph Metzelder has since picked up runners-up medals from the UEFA Cup and World Cup in 2002 – then Euro 2008. Metzelder rose to prominence at Dortmund in 2000. Within two years he had cemented his place in the national team and in 2007 he ignored overtures from Manchester United and signed for Real Madrid, who he helped win La Liga in his first season. Tall and strong in the air, Metzelder plays predominantly in the centre of defence but his tackling ability also makes him a useful full-back.

John Obi Mikel
Nigeria

DoB	22 April 1987
Height	1.80m
Weight	80kg
Position	Midfielder
Nigeria	19 caps
	2 goals
Chelsea	51 league games
	0 goals
Transfer fee	£16million

Uncompromising Nigerian John Obi Mikel forced his way in to Chelsea's star-studded midfield after a protracted transfer and played all 120 minutes of the 2008 Champions League final. A fierce competitor with solid passing skills and impressive stamina, Obi was wanted by both Chelsea and Manchester United after impressing as an 18-year-old for Norwegian side Lyn Oslo and at the 2006 African Nations Cup. He signed deals with both of the English clubs – the United contract without his agents' presence. To settle the ongoing dispute that followed, Chelsea finally agreed to pay their Premier League rivals £12million, and Lyn £4million.

Gabriel Milito
Argentina

DoB	7 September 1980
Height	1.86m
Weight	84kg
Position	Defender
Argentina	32 caps
	1 goal
Barcelona	27 league games
	1 goal
Transfer fee	£13.53million

When Barcelona face Real Zaragoza in Spain's La Liga this season it won't be the fist time Gabriel Milito has played against brother Diego in competitive action. The pair faced each other in the Argentine First Division, Gabriel at Independiente, Diego at Racing Club, before they became team-mates at Zaragoza in 2003. After four seasons he became the 20th Argentine to join Catalan giants Barca. The 27-year-old defender scored his first league goal against Recreativo Huelva in November 2007, but a cruciate ligament injury sidelined him for six months. He has represented Argentina at the 2005 Confederations Cup and 2006 World Cup.

Luka Modric
Croatia

DoB	9 September 1985
Height	1.73m
Weight	65kg
Position	Midfielder
Croatia	29 caps
	4 goals
Tottenham Hotspur	0 league games
	0 goals
Transfer fee	£16.5million

Tottenham Hotspur equalled their record transfer when they paid £16.5million for Luka Modric in 2008. The Croatian schemer played in both defeats of England in the Euro 2008 qualifiers and was voted Player of the Year in 2007 by his peers, following in the footsteps of Niko Kranjcar and Eduardo da Silva. He was subsequently awarded a 10-year contract by Dinamo Zagreb following successful loan spells with Zrinjski Mostar and Inter Zapresic. A move to England proved tempting, however. "I leave with beautiful memories," he said on his departure; he'll be hoping to create many more in north London.

Adrian Mutu
Romania

DoB	8 January 1979
Height	1.80m
Weight	74kg
Position	Striker
Romania	64 caps
	29 goals
Fiorentina	62 league games
	33 goals
Transfer fee	£5.54million

A streak of 18 goals in 18 games for Dinamo Bucharest convinced Inter Milan to pay €6.5million for Adrian Mutu in 2000 – but when the sleek Romanian international failed to score in 10 games for the Nerazzurri, his top-class career looked in doubt. A move to Verona reignited Mutu's form, prompting Parma to shell out €10m for his services – and within a year Chelsea paid more than twice that fee to take him to London. Mutu was sacked after failing a drugs test and returned to Italy to rebuild his career with Juventus before making a £5.54m switch to his eighth club, Fiorentina, in 2006.

Nani
Portugal

DoB	17 November 1986
Height	1.75m
Weight	66kg
Position	Midfielder
Portugal	16 caps
	2 goals
Manchester	26 league games
United	3 goals
Transfer fee	£17million

Nani follows in the footsteps of Luis Figo, Hugo Viana and Cristiano Ronaldo in graduating from Sporting Lisbon's impressive youth academy. The young winger followed Ronaldo to Manchester United and announced his arrival at Old Trafford with a spectacular winning goal against Tottenham Hotspur – earning his side's first victory of their Double-winning season and celebrating with an impressive back-flip to boot. "We're quite bullish about him," beamed United manager Sir Alex Ferguson of his new capture. "He's very quick and a marvellous crosser." His former national coach agrees – "Nani could b [Luis] Figo's heir," suggested Luiz Felipe Scolari ahead of Euro 2008.

Samir Nasri
France

DoB	20 June 1987
Height	1.77m
Weight	75kg
Position	Midfielder
France	12 caps
	2 goals
Arsenal	0 league games
	0 goals
Transfer fee	£11.93million

It didn't take long for attacking midfielder Samir Nasri to be compared to French maestro Zinedine Zidane. The two share Algerian roots – and many believe the young playmaker can emulate Zidane's success for Les Bleus. Nasri made his Marseille debut aged just 17 and in 2007, at the end of his fourth season, he was voted Ligue 1's Young Player of the Year. In the summer of 2008 he joined Arsenal, having represented his country at every level, from the under 16s to the full national team. He has 12 full caps and has already scored two goals.

Ivica Olic
Croatia

DoB	14 September 1979
Height	1.82m
Weight	82kg
Position	Striker
Croatia	57 caps
	10 goals
Hamburger SV	47 league games
	19 goals
Transfer fee	£1.31million

Born finisher Ivica Olic has scored goals everywhere he has played and proved he's one of the most hard-working strikers around at Euro 2008. He began at Marsonia and rejoined the club after struggling to break into the Hertha Berlin team as a teenager. After 38 goals in 84 games, Olic was loaned to NK Zagreb, where he rattled in 21 goals in a single season before representing Dinamo Zagreb (16 in 27) and CSKA Moscow (35 in 78) to earn a move back to the Bundesliga. In October 2007, Olic became the first player in Hamburg's history to score a first-half hat-trick.

Rodrigo Palacio
Argentina

DoB	5 February 1982
Height	1.75m
Weight	66kg
Position	Forward
Argentina	8 caps
	1 goal
Boca	110 league games
Juniors	50 goals
Transfer fee	n/a

Rodrigo Palacio has won six titles with Argentine giants Boca Juniors; no surprise, then, that the 26-year-old forward fancies a new challenge. "If I do not go now then later on it could be difficult for me and Boca will not receive the best price for me," he told reporters in the summer of 2008. His career started at Huracan de Tres Arroyos in 2002. A move to Banfield followed before Boca signed him in 2005. His impressive performances alerted Argentine coach Jose Pekerman and he scored his first international goal against Ecuador in June 2008 in a World Cup qualifier.

Roman Pavlyuchenko
Russia

DoB	15 December 1981
Height	1.88m
Weight	78kg
Position	Striker
Russia	22 caps
	9 goals
Spartak Moscow	136 league games
	67 goals
Transfer fee	Undisclosed

Two goals in four second-half minutes against England in the Euro 2008 qualifiers truly put Roman Pavlyuchenko firmly in the spotlight. Before that game, a crucial 2–1 victory, the clinical finisher was virtually unknown outside his homeland. After starting his league career at Rotor Volgograd, Pavlyuchenko moved to Spartak Moscow ahead of the 2003 season and won the Russian Cup in his first season with the capital club. Twice leading goalscorer in the Russian Premier-Liga since then, Pavlyuchenko was named in UEFA's team of the tournament after scoring four goals in his country's march to the Euro 2008 semi-finals.

Alexandre Pato
Brazil

DoB	1 September 1989
Height	1.79m
Weight	71kg
Position	Striker
Brazil	3 caps
	1 goal
AC Milan	18 league games
	9 goals
Transfer fee	£14.82million

Alexandre Rodrigues da Silva is a Brazilian striker who boasts a similar playing style to Ronaldo. Born in Pato Branco – which translates as white duck, Pato's nickname – he scored a goal every two games in Serie A last season after making his AC Milan debut midway through the campaign. He started his career at Sport Club Internacional in 2001 and made his debut aged just 17 in 2006 against Sociedade Esportiva Palmeiras. He scored one and set up the other three in a 4–1 win. His electric pace alerted Europe's biggest clubs and he signed for the Rossoneri in August 2007.

Pepe
Portugal

DoB	26 February 1983
Height	1.86m
Weight	72kg
Position	Defender
Portugal	7 caps
	1 goal
Real Madrid	19 league games
	0 goals
Transfer fee	£20million

Brazilian-born Pepe – who was granted Portuguese citizenship in August 2007 – made his international debut in Portugal's final Euro 2008 qualifier at home to Finland before starring at the tournament itself. His stock had already risen after he'd helped Real Madrid win the Primera Division title in his first season at the Bernabeu, having joined the club from Porto a year earlier. Pepe won two successive league titles with Porto in 2005/06 and 2006/07 after joining the Portuguese giants from CS Maritimo, where his commitment and ever-ready smile made him a popular figure with the fans.

Mladen Petric
Croatia

DoB	1 January 1981
Height	1.83m
Weight	79kg
Position	Striker
Croatia	27 caps
	9 goals
Borussia	29 league games
Dortmund	13 goals
Transfer fee	Undisclosed

Averaging a goal every three games for his country, Petric became the first Croatian to score four times in a competitive match when he helped them crush Andorra 7–0 in 2006. His winning goal at Wembley in November 2007 prevented England from qualifying for Euro 2008, but he went on to miss the decisive penalty in Croatia's quarter-final shoot-out defeat against Turkey in Vienna. Petric began his professional career with FC Baden before he was signed by Grasshoppers Zurich and later FC Basel, where he won a league and cup double. He now plays for Borussia Dortmund in the Bundesliga.

Fabio Quagliarella
Italy

ITALIA

FIGC

DoB	31 January 1983
Height	1.82m
Weight	73kg
Position	Striker
Italy	8 caps
	3 goals
Udinese	37 league games
	12 goals
Transfer fee	£4.87million

Despite only making his first league start in 2002, powerhouse forward Fabio Quagliarella has already represented six clubs – and found the net for all of them. Once part-owned by three different Serie A clubs, Quagliarella was sent out on loan by cash-strapped Torino but showed no signs of being unsettled by the string of moves. His 13 goals for Sampdoria and classy double for Italy in a Euro 2008 qualifier against Lithuania convinced Udinese to pay almost £5million for the striker, who can also play out wide in midfield – and is never afraid to shoot from distance.

Ivan Rakitic
Croatia

DoB	10 March 1988
Height	1.84m
Weight	72kg
Position	Midfielder
Croatia	11 caps
	1 goal
Schalke 04	3 league games
	29 goals
Transfer fee	Free

One of several Croatians playing in Germany's Bundesliga, midfielder Ivan Rakitic started his career at FC Basel in Switzerland, where he was named best young player in 2006/07. Rakitic left the country he'd represented at under-21 level to join FC Schalke 04 in 2007, scoring three league goals in his debut season. His first strike for the club came in a 9-0 German Cup win over Eintracht Trier and he scored for his country on his second appearance, against Andorra in a Euro 2008 qualifier. His impressive tournament displays made him a target for some of Europe's biggest clubs.

Sergio Ramos
Spain

DoB	30 March 1986
Height	1.83m
Weight	73kg
Position	Defender
Spain	39 caps
	4 goals
Real Madrid	99 league games
	14 goals
Transfer fee	£18.48million

A fee approaching £20million seems a lot to pay for a teenager, but that's exactly what Real Madrid did when they took swashbuckling centre-half Sergio Ramos to the Bernabeu Stadium in August 2005. Nurtured – originally as a striker – by his local side Sevilla, Ramos made just 39 La Liga appearances for the Rojiblancos before Madrid made their move. Since the switch, the defender has formed a solid partnership with Fabio Cannavaro and helped Los Merengues win back-to-back La Liga titles. Despite only being 22, the Euro 2008 final victory over Germany marked Ramos' 39th international cap.

Micah Richards
England

DoB	24 June 1988
Height	1.80m
Weight	83kg
Position	Defender
England	11 caps
	1 goal
Manchester City	66 league games
	1 goal
Transfer fee	n/a

ENGLAND

"I have not worked with anyone so good," said former Manchester City boss Stuart Pearce shortly before leaving the club where Richards is found either at right back or in the centre of defence. The versatile defender has risen to prominence with a series of assured performances for club and country and has been a target for a number of top teams. Richards recently committed his future to the Eastlands outfit until 2013, having been voted City's Young Player of the Year in 2006. He made his international debut in November that year, against Holland, to become England's youngest ever defender.

Robinho
Brazil

DoB	25 January 1984
Height	1.72m
Weight	60kg
Position	Forward
Brazil	55 caps
	13 goals
Real Madrid	101 league games
	25 goals
Transfer fee	£16.64million

The 24-year-old signed for Real Madrid in 2005 after spending three years with Brazilian club Santos. Yet despite scoring 25 goals in 101 La Liga appearances, he was never guaranteed a regular starting place in Los Blancos' first XI. Robinho's form at Santos brought nine goals in 24 games in his debut season as his side won the Campeonato Brasileiro. Two years later he scored 21 goals in 37 league games to help secure the title again before his move to Spain. He earned his first Brazilian cap in 2003 and has scored 13 goals in 55 internationals.

Tomas Rosicky
Czech Republic

DoB	4 October 1980
Height	1.78m
Weight	67kg
Position	Midfielder
Czech Republic	68 caps
	19 goals
Arsenal	44 league games
	9 goals
Transfer fee	£6.8million

Nicknamed 'Little Mozart', Tomas Rosicky is an attacking midfielder with an eye for a killer pass. Leaving first club Sparta Prague in 2001 he cost new employers Borussia Dortmund a then Bundesliga record fee of £18million. He proved he was worth every penny, scoring 20 goals in 149 league appearances before joining Arsenal in 2006, where he assumed the No.7 shirt left behind by the departing Robert Pires. Deployed on the left wing, Rosicky has scored just nine goals in two seasons, but his form was enough to make him Czech Republic captain. Unfortunately, he missed Euro 2008 with a knee injury.

Simão Sabrosa
Portugal

DoB	30 October 1979
Height	1.70m
Weight	64kg
Position	Forward
Portugal	64 caps
	15 goals
Atletico Madrid	30 league games
	7 goals
Transfer fee	£14million

Simão Sabrosa stated his career with Sporting Lisbon, scored on his debut in 1996/97 and went on to bag a further 11 goals in 52 league appearances before moving to Barcelona in 1999. But it was back at Benfica in 2001 that he became an instant favourite. The club captain was Benfica's highest scorer for six consecutive seasons, with 95 goals in 230 all-competition matches. Unsurprisingly, he was linked with a host of clubs in 2007 but insisted: "I'm a Benfica player and that is the end of it," before promptly signing for Atletico Madrid. He scored seven goals in his debut campaign.

Bacary Sagna
France

DoB	14 February 1983
Height	1.76m
Weight	72kg
Position	Defender
France	2 caps
	0 goals
Arsenal	29 league games
	1 goals
Transfer fee	£6million

When Bacary Sagna signed for Arsenal in July 2007, few had heard of the Sens-born full-back. Yet in France he had already developed a fine reputation while impressing in his 87 appearances for Auxerre. He was part of the squad that won the French Cup in 2005 and before joining the Gunners, Sagna finished in the Ligue 1 team of the season. He continued where he left off and was named in the PFA team of the year after his first year in England. Sagna – with two caps – often forced regular right full-back Emmanuel Eboue into a more attacking role.

Tuncay Sanli
Turkey

DoB	16 January 1982
Height	1.82m
Weight	70kg
Position	Forward
Turkey	58 caps
	15 goals
Middlesbrough	34 league games
	8 goals
Transfer fee	Free

Middlesbrough's Tuncay Sanli was one of the key players behind Turkey's surprise progress at Euro 2008. The former Fenerbahce forward helped his country reach the last four with shock victories over the Czech Republic and Croatia, but was forced to sit out their semi-final defeat to Germany through suspension. Tuncay scored 59 goals in 154 league games for Fenerbahce before joining Boro on a Bosman free transfer in 2007. He was an instant hit at the Riverside, scoring eight times in his first Premier League season – and his value will only have increased after Turkey's stunning European Championship run.

Roque Santa Cruz
Paraguay

DoB	16 August 1981
Height	1.89m
Weight	80kg
Position	Striker
Paraguay	61 caps
	20 goals
Blackburn	37 league games
	19 goals
Transfer fee	£3.5million

Named Paraguayan player of the year shortly after his 18th birthday, Roque Santa Cruz had already made his international debut and moved from Olimpia Asuncion to Bayern Munich. The striker – an elegant player blessed with pace and clinical finishing – spent eight seasons with the German giants, helping the club win five Bundesliga titles and four German cups. Former Premier League champions Blackburn paid £3.5million for the centre-forward in July 2007 and he rewarded them by producing the best football of his career so far, rattling in 19 goals in his first season at Ewood Park.

Marcos Senna
Spain

DoB	17 July 1976
Height	1.77m
Weight	68kg
Position	Midfielder
Spain	16 caps
	0 goals
Villarreal	150 league games
	11 goals
Transfer fee	n/a

A tireless midfielder with supreme passing skills and an eye for goal, Marcos Senna was the driving force behind Spain's triumph at Euro 2008. Born in Rio de Janeiro, he was granted Spanish citizenship in 2006, by which time he had won the FIFA Club World Cup with Corinthians, one of the five teams he represented in Brazil, and moved to La Liga. Despite arriving in Europe at a later stage of his career than many high-profile South Americans, Senna quickly cemented his place in the Villarreal midfield, even scoring from inside the centre-circle in one game against Real Betis.

David Silva
Spain

DoB	8 January 1986
Height	1.72m
Weight	67kg
Position	Midfielder
Spain	19 caps
	3 goals
Valencia	70 league games
	9 goals
Transfer fee	n/a

Spotted playing football on the Canary Islands by Valencia scouts in 2001, attacking midfielder David Silva has developed into one of Spanish football's hottest youngsters. The Spanish international, who loves to use both feet and cut inside from either flank, earned his spurs on season-long loans at Eibar and Celta Vigo before establishing himself as part of the furniture at the Mestalla. Part of the Spain team which won the European Under-19 Championship in 2004, Silva graduated to the national team in November 2006. The sought-after star made five appearances on the left flank for Spain at Euro 2008.

Ebi Smolarek
Poland

DoB	9 January 1981
Height	1.78m
Weight	68kg
Position	Striker
Poland	34 caps
	13 goals
Racing	34 league games
Santander	4 goals
Transfer fee	£3.25million

Named after Portuguese legend Eusebio, football was always in the blood for Euzebiusz 'Ebi' Smolarek. Son of Wlodzimerz Smolarek, who played for Poland in two World Cups in the 1980s, Ebi was brought up in Holland and signed for Feyenoord as a teenager. Four seasons at the De Kuip stadium brought only one trophy – the 2002 UEFA Cup – although Smolarek was suspended for the showcase against Borussia Dortmund. Coincidentally, he joined the German side in 2005, and scored 25 goals for the Schwarzgelben before making his 2007 move to Racing Santander, who often deploy the fleet-footed forward as a winger.

Eduardo da Silva
Croatia

DoB	25 February 1983
Height	1.77m
Weight	73kg
Position	Striker
Croatia	22 caps
	13 goals
Arsenal	17 league games
	4 goals
Transfer fee	£8.5million

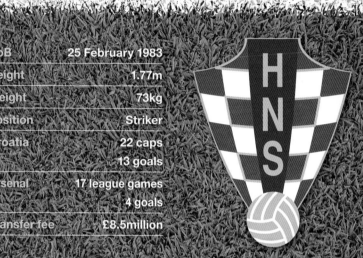

Brazilian-born Croatian Eduardo da Silva returns to action this season following an horrific ankle injury sustained against Birmingham City in February 2008. The clinical finisher joined Arsenal in the summer of 2007 after helping Dinamo Zagreb to consecutive league titles. He was voted Croatia's Player of the Year three years out of four and in his final season at Dinamo, he scored 34 goals in 32 games, breaking a 13-year-old record set by former Dinamo Modri striker Goran Vlaovic (29 goals). He signed off with a hat-trick against local rivals Hadjuk Split, the first player to do so in the derby.

Wesley Sneijder
Holland

DoB	9 June 1984
Height	1.70m
Weight	67kg
Position	Midfielder
Holland	48 caps
	11 goals
Real Madrid	30 league games
	9 goals
Transfer fee	£20million

KNVB

Creative midfielder Wesley Sneijder's rise can be charted
by his contrasting fortunes in the 2004 and 2008 European
Championships. In Portugal in 2004 Sneijder was no more than
a fringe player, but in Austria and Switzerland four years later
he impressed and scored two terrific goals in three games.
Sneijder helped Ajax to the 2003/04 Eredivisie title, then won
back-to-back Dutch Cups in 2006 and 2007 before Real Madrid
shelled out £20million for his services. A two-footed midfielder
with a fierce shot, Sneijder proved his class as Real won their
31st La Liga title in his first season at the Bernabeu.

Alexandre Song
Cameroon

DoB	9 April 1987
Height	1.82m
Weight	76kg
Position	Midfielder
Cameroon	11 caps
	0 goals
Arsenal	16 league games
	0 goals
Transfer fee	£1million

A central midfielder by trade, Alexandre Song ended the 2007/08 campaign impressing in the centre of Arsenal's defence. Song joined the Gunners on a permanent deal in 2006 from French club Bastia after impressing during a year-long loan. He made his debut in September 2005 against Everton – but had to wait a further 16 months for his first goal, which came in a league cup tie against Liverpool. In January 2007 he joined Charlton Athletic on loan. They were relegated later that year, but Song became a Cameroon regular during the African Nations Cup and was named in the team of the tournament.

Gabriel Tamas
Romania

DoB	18 November 1983
Height	1.88m
Weight	77kg
Position	Defender
Romania	35 caps
	2 goals
Auxerre	27 league games
	0 goals
Transfer fee	Undisclosed

Auxerre endured their worst campaign for six years in 2007/08 but one enormous positive was the emergence of former Romania Under-21 captain Gabriel Tamas as a world-class defender. The aerially gifted centre-half has learned to read the game, having gained Champions League experience during a short spell with Galatasaray and having played against some of the world's greatest strikers on a season-long loan at Spanish side Celta Vigo. Now seemingly settled at Auxerre, Tamas flourished for his country at Euro 2008, helping Romania hold the might of France and Italy with unwavering, solid displays at the back.

Carlos Tevez
Argentina

DoB	5 February 1984
Height	1.73m
Weight	74kg
Position	Striker
Argentina	40 caps
	7 goals
Manchester United	34 league games
	14 goals
Transfer fee	Undisclosed

Soon after his winning goal at Old Trafford kept West Ham United in the Premiership in 2006/07, Manchester United moved swiftly to sign the Argentine striker's registration from the Media Sports Investments consortium. The settlement deal took several weeks, but Tevez repaid his new club with a number of crucial last-minute goals and a series of tireless displays as United secured a 17th league title and third European Cup triumph. Tevez began his football education on the Fuerte Apachen streets of Buenos Aires. He was spotted by Boca Juniors, where one goal every three games saw him move to Corinthians before his move to West Ham in 2006.

Luca Toni
Italy

DoB	26 May 1977
Height	1.93m
Weight	88kg
Position	Striker
Italy	38 caps
	15 goals
Bayern Munich	31 league games
	24 goals
Transfer fee	£7.46million

Strapping centre-forward Luca Toni is Italy's first-choice striker – but took his time getting there. The journeyman began his career at Modena, polished his skills alongside Roberto Baggio at Brescia but only truly established himself when he joined his eighth club, Palermo, in 2003. He scored 31 league goals to help the Rosanero back to Serie A for the first time since 1973. A €10million switch to Fiorentina saw Toni win the European golden shoe for his 31-goal haul and in the summer of 2007 he completed an €11million move to Bayern Munich, scoring 24 goals in his first Bundesliga season.

Dmitri Torbinski
Russia

DoB	28 April 1984
Height	1.72m
Weight	60kg
Position	Midfielder
Russia	14 caps
	2 goals
Lokomotiv Moscow	10 league games
	1 goal
Transfer fee	Undisclosed

Dmitri Torbinski secured his place in Russian folklore when he put his country ahead in the dying stages of their Euro 2008 quarter-final against Holland, stabbing in Andrei Arshavin's left-wing delivery with the outside of his boot to floor the Dutch. The versatile winger – equally comfortable supplying crosses as finishing them – suffered serious cruciate knee ligament damage in 2004. The recovery process was long, managing only 19 games for Spartak Moscow by the end of 2006. But after helping Spartak finish second in the Premier-Liga in 2007, Torbinski joined Lokomotiv and became a regular for Guus Hiddink's Russia.

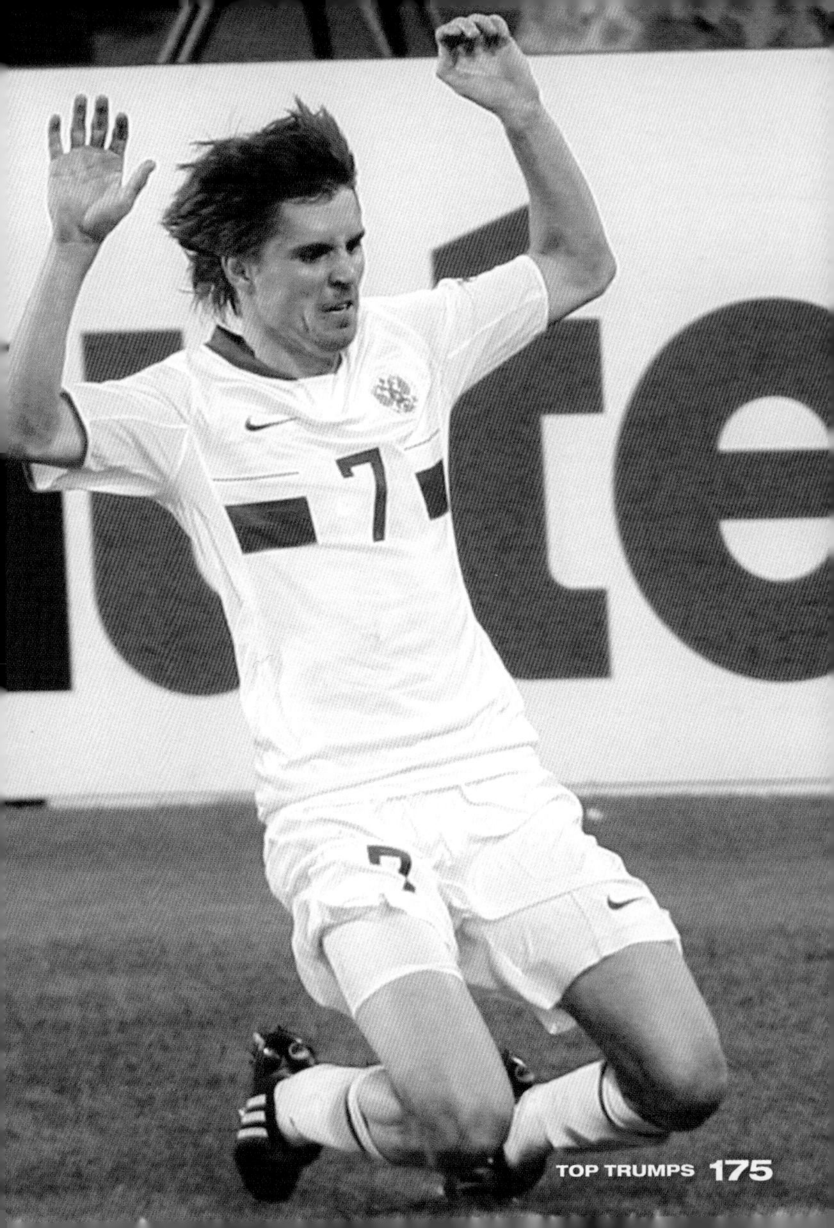

Yaya Toure
Ivory Coast

DoB	13 May 1983
Height	1.87m
Weight	78kg
Position	Defender
Ivory Coast	29 caps
	3 goals
Barcelona	26 league games
	1 goal
Transfer fee	£6.06million

A tireless runner with precise passing skills, Barcelona's Yaya Toure is arguably Barcelona's most valuable holding midfielder since current manager Josep Guardiola was playing at the Nou Camp. Having helped the Ivory Coast reach their first World Cup finals in 2006, the younger brother of Arsenal's Kolo Toure joined Monaco from Shakhtar Donetsk. One impressive season in France – with five goals from 24 Ligue 1 starts – earned Toure a £6.06million move to Barcelona and in his first season, he helped the Catalan side reach the semi-finals of the Champions League, where they were edged out by eventual winners Manchester United.

Robin van Persie
Holland

DoB	6 August 1983
Height	1.82m
Weight	69kg
Position	Forward
Holland	28 caps
	9 goals
Arsenal	87 league games
	28 goals
Transfer fee	£3million

KNVB

Despite disciplinary problems as a youngster, Robin van Persie won the UEFA Cup in his first season at Feyenoord, playing a star role in the final against Borussia Dortmund. Van Persie joined Arsenal for £3million in 2004 and, despite enduring a succession of injuries, his finishing skills have made him one of the most elegant and clinical strikers in the Premier League. He won the FA Cup in his first season – scoring twice in the semi-final against Blackburn Rovers – before helping the north London club reach the Champions League final the following season.

Rafael van der Vaart

Holland

DoB	11 February 1983
Height	1.74m
Weight	70kg
Position	Midfielder
Holland	58 caps
	12 goals
Hamburg	74 league games
	29 goals
Transfer fee	£5.2million

KNVB

Rafael van der Vaart has suffered from a series of injuries throughout his career – never managing more than 28 league starts in a season – but the left-footed star nevertheless had 50 caps before his 25th birthday. He made his professional bow at Ajax aged just 17 after impressing for the youth team. In 2001/02 he rattled in 14 league goals before a knee injury curtailed his season. The playmaker returned a year later with 18 goals and in 2003/04 he helped Ajax to another title. His solid form and dependable goalscoring record have continued since his switch to the Bundesliga in 2005.

Theo Walcott
England

DoB	16 March 1989
Height	1.76m
Weight	68kg
Position	Forward
England	2 caps
	0 goals
Arsenal	41 league games
	4 goals
Transfer fee	£5million

ENGLAND

Signed by Southampton from Swindon Town in 2004, Theo Walcott soon showed the Robins what they were missing. He starred in Saints' FA Youth Cup winning team of 2005 and became Southampton's youngest-ever first team player at 16 years and 143 days of age. A string of electric performances and one spectacular chipped goal against Luton alerted Arsenal to his potential. Walcott joined the north London club in January 2006, became the youngest ever full England international at the age of 17 years and 75 days in a 3–1 win against Hungary and, after a slow start, established himself in the Gunners first team.

Jonathan Woodgate
England

ENGLAND

DoB	22 January 1980
Height	1.87m
Weight	80kg
Position	Defender
England	7 caps
	0 goals
Tottenham Hotspur	12 league games
	1 goal
Transfer fee	£8million

Sturdy centre-half Jonathan Woodgate left first club Leeds United in 2003 after more than 100 appearances and showed signs of promise at Newcastle United, who he soon left to join Real Madrid. He scored an own goal and was sent off on his Real debut, but he soon became something of a cult hero – despite only making nine appearances in an injury-plagued spell at the Bernabeu. He then joined hometown club Middlesbrough, first on loan and then permanently in 2007, before helping Spurs to the 2008 League Cup – the north London club's first trophy in nine years – only months after an £8million switch.

Ashley Young
England

DoB	9 July 1985
Height	1.75m
Weight	63kg
Position	Forward
England	3 caps
	0 goals
Aston Villa	50 league games
	10 goals
Transfer fee	£8million

England international Ashley Young's persistence as a young footballer paid off when, after initially being rejected by Watford, he earned a second chance that saw him break into the first team as an 18-year-old. In 2004/05 Young was named Watford's best young player – the following season a haul of 13 goals in 39 appearances helped the Hornets win promotion to the Premier League, where his scintillating form continued. Aston Villa fought off a number of clubs to secure his signature in January 2007, and he has rewarded them with 10 Premier League goals and a steady supply of assists from the wing.

Yuri Zhirkov
Russia

DoB	20 August 1983
Height	1.78m
Weight	70kg
Position	Midfielder
Russia	24 caps
	0 goals
CSKA Moscow	111 league games
	11 goals
Transfer fee	Undisclosed

CSKA Moscow's UEFA Cup triumph in 2005 brought rapid left midfielder Yuri Zhirkov to the attention of a global audience. The left-footed player had already helped his side bag the first of two back-to-back Russian Premier-Liga titles when he hit what proved to be the winning goal against Sporting Lisbon to seal the Army Men's first European trophy. A hard-running player unafraid to track back and defend, Zhirkov played played all five games for his country as Russia swept through to the semi-finals at Euro 2008 – and was rewarded with a place in UEFA's team of the tournament.